Cycles

Shantel S

Presentation by *BookLeaf Publishing*

Web: www.bookleafpub.com

E-mail: info@bookleafpub.com

ISBN: 9789357215053

First edition 2022

More

I'm so scared of change
Of moving on
Of letting go
But something in me tells me there has to be
more
The love that I'm receiving?
I deserve more.
I know that I can feel so much more for
someone
But I haven't found them yet
Maybe that's where fear kicks in
What if they never turn up?

Gift Wrapped

I gave my heart, gift-wrapped
to someone who didn't even have the decency to
open the box
What makes you any different?
What makes you worth it?
What makes you think that after all the pain
there was a possibility?

Love

People don't love love
People love the power
People love the kind gestures and compliments
the butterflies and the heart warming intimacy
that love comes with.
People reap the benefits of love
but are never willing to give as much as they are
receiving.
Love requires you to give, give all of you
give so much you forget to take
Love is when keeping someone else happy is the
method to your own happiness
Love
Love is reckless
unpredictable and far from mediocre

52016

She pulled emotions out of me like she was
searching for a missing shoe
Throwing my pride to the side because it didn't
match
I reached for it, placing it in a box
This time not under lock and key
This time not hiding behind it
Throwing my anxiety behind the heater
Heating it to the point of uneasiness
My mouth dried as my heart began to race
Was this really happening?
As I reached to save 'us' from an explosion of
emotions
She reached in to pull out my patience
I yelled internally as I seemed to lose 'it'
I felt the edges of my expectations cut like a
knife as it protruded my skin
I bit my lip to hide the pain
Which she perceived as a look of sultry
It seemed to urge her on as she grabbed my
pensiveness
Mingling it with hers and fusing them together
as one
Apprehension was the next to go

All my doubts and fears seemed to leave my
body as if waiting for this very moment
Next was my peace of mind
My eyes watered as I realized there was no more
me
Just Us

Sun I Am

You're like the sun and
I am hopelessly drawn towards you
Skin burning to a crisp but
I reach for you
My very existence nearing the end as
You absorb every dust particle
But I am the Sun
Not like
So we become one
Leaving a trail of fire in our wake

Bonfire

I have these flashbacks where we're in my car
your curls are dancing around your face
I glance over at you
just in time to see your lips say
I love you
It's like a movie playing on repeat
I try to remember each and every detail of the
scene.
I see your brown eyes look at me in such
certainty.
It's almost in slow motion.
Your lips turn upright in such a knowing smile
As if you know just what those words do
Creating a bonfire in the pit of my heart
Begging you to stay
Urging you to seek refuge
Here with me

Existential

They
Say everything happens
For a reason
But enclose the reason
In a present called
Future
Cause
Only time will tell
But why bring so many
Dark manipulating clouds all at once?
Why leave lingering thoughts and question when
no one can even answer
them
And if that someone
Up above
Loves us so unconditionally
How can he sit
And watch us hurt so much
Some beg and
Plead
For a better life
But never receive
I live
Love
Laugh

Hurt
Haunt and
Helplessly
Keep my head
Up.

Collision

Something so profound and delicate is what I
feel for you
A feeling questioned continuously to how much
I really care
Because of a lack in one specific area I gain
extradinary and unreliable
emotions that I helplessy find a need to hide
Wondering what's best for you and if my love is
enough
Yes love
Not like
Not lust
Love
Is my love enough for such beauty indescribable
and breathtaking
What is my love even worth to you?
Do you even know about my love?
Do I even exist to you?

Fate

With a smile so irresistable
You stand
With a piece of me
In your hand
And I let it be
Because
A friend said it was fate
And I said
Lets just wait
And see
How quick
I get hurt
And yet I don't
Regret letting
it happen
Atleast
Untill
I get hurt
And a touch so temptin
I push you away but keep
Hoping you
Come right back
And you do
And yeah I
Front

But like
What else can I do
Wen something so forbidden
Keeps me
Wishing and wanting
More...

Watermelon

We have a companionship like no other
Well I'd like to believe that
But who's to say God would only bless me,
of all people,
with a companion like you.
With someone with lips like a slice of
watermelon.
Wait maybe that was a bad comparison.
Now I seem like the typical black person, while
on the contrary I don't like watermelon.
But if watermelon tasted like your lips baby I'd
eat it all day.
But lemme break it down to you.
Lips like watermelon.
So red and so juicy.
So full and so addicting.
So refreshing on an any type of day.
Get it?
Good.
With someone so breathtaking you make
complements that wash over me,
blinding me,
making me see what you see in me through your
eyes.
So amazing,

I never want to leave you.
You make it so easy to laugh with you,
talk with you.
Be open with you.
Like God said
"Here, I'm sorry you were so lonely".
 love spending time with you.
Being with you.
Crying with you.
Just talking to you about anything. T
o be able to do nothing, something or
everything.
You're there when I need you
and even when
I just want you.

52816

Her back arched as my lips began to taste her
skin
Her caramel skin meshed with my Hershey tone
like the foam gathered on hot chocolate
disturbed.
As I inched up to taste her lips I could hear the
tension in the air
Like static it shocked us both out of reality
Her hands seem to roam faster than I could
anticipate as we fought for dominance
It was my turn to give
My turn to show
My turn to love
I straddled her thighs faster than she could
register
Her instant gasp formed a pull in my stomach
As she tried to reach for me I pulled away
watching a frown form on her beautiful face
I could have given in, but the sight of her naked
body tore my attention away from my pouting
baby
She deserved this
She earned this
I was hers and I'd prove it
Our tongues intertwined

As she gripped my hair, my hand around her
throat
Our tongues moved like two dance partners
Knowing the others moves but still being
surprised by the efficiency
I ran my hand down her body in an effort to feel
all of her all at once
I just couldn't get enough
In a split second I was on my back looking at an
evil smirk
Now it was my turn to gasp and pout
But it didn't last for long as she reached for my
lips
Kissing and sucking like she was grasping for
air
I fought for the upper hand even while having a
less advantage of winning
As I licked her lips, the contact of my piercing
being her weakness
I watched devilishly as she looked down at me
ready to devour
Hooking my leg to the bottom of the bed I
slipped down to between her legs
Before she could even react my lips found her
clit
Greeted with juices I got to work
Reminding her I was in control
She was mine tonight

Crushed

But I've died too
And I don't know what new person opened her
eyes
I only know what she has been
what she has lost
and the weight of it is almost
crushing

Got Love?

I learned that I can't expect someone
Hurt and broken to treat me right
When they don't even know how to treat
themselves
I'd be siking myself out
If I sit here and give you
all this love that you can't return to me,
when that's all I need
I need you to love me and
feel me and
adore me
but you don't know how because you've only
ever been hurt
So it escapes me when
you say you've been in love
How could you have been
in love but you don't understand that
when I say I want an apology I want more.
I want you to show me how apologetic you are.
How could you have been in
love yet you allow your
past to take over and decipher your future?
How could you possibly love me, when you
don't even love yourself?

Burned

They will tell you they love you
but give it a few months or so
and they'll extinguish the fire
they put in you just to burn someone else

Hold On

I know this transformation is painful
but you're not falling apart
you're just falling into something different
with a new capacity
to be beautiful
to be refreshed
to be renewed
to reach depths unthinkable
hold on

Sprung

I wanna believe everything you tell me is the
truth.
Willingly each word is hidden in my heart
With no light or impact of
what others may think or say.
Anyone with a motive to hurt me has fought a
battle with
No one but you
Your tranquilized affection leaves me lost but
what's new
Your desirable wants leave me wanting to please
you in any way
possible
Outright sprung and obsessed is what I am for
you
Unfortunately there's nothing I can do

Friends

I messed up when I caught feelings for you
I knew from the beginning you would only
destroy me
I knew you couldn't be what I needed you to be
But you were so tempting.
So alluring.
I said fuck it.
This should have only been a friendship.
& God.
It would have been the best friendship of your
life.
It has been the best friendship of your life.
I've allowed you to get in touch with
sides of you,
you've forgotten about
and have been running from
I was your laugh when there was no joke
your shoulder when there was no tissue
I wiped your tears
I've made you laugh only seconds after being in
a heated argument with me
Baby who else you know can do that to you?
I've watched your eyes brighten at the thought of
a definite future.

Watched your smile take me off into a place of
love.
I've loved you.
Loved you.
Loved you in every way I know how.
I've brought you to my family,
my church,
my sanctuary.
I've given you thoughts that I haven't shared
with the world
Memories that may be hard to ever forget.
I've reminded you of your worth
Now you're realizing you deserve better then me
Because I knew once I laid eyes on you a
goddess lived in your soul
and was only figuring a way to get out.
I've always felt so unworthy of your loving but it
turns out it was you that was unworthy of my
loving.

Selfish

I've found it much easier to end things lately
much easier to be truthful with what I want
Declaring this is what I want and Im sorry if that
hurts you or
I come off detached,
but I've spent years giving and doing
what I don't want
For all the wrong reasons
or out of respect
I'm done
Call me
Selfish